MATH MADE EASY

3rd Grade Workbook

10 Minutes A Day
Multiplication

Consultant Alison Tribley

10-minute challenge

Try to complete the exercises for each topic in 10 minutes or less. Note the time it takes you in the "Time taken" column below.

DK London
Editor Elizabeth Blakemore
Senior Editor Deborah Lock
US Editor Allison Singer
US Math Consultant Alison Tribley
Managing Editor Christine Stroyan
Managing Art Editor Anna Hall
Senior Production Editor Andy Hilliard
Senior Production Controller Jude Crozier
Jacket Design Development Manager Sophia MTT
Publisher Andrew Macintyre
Associate Publishing Director Liz Wheeler
Art Director Karen Self
Publishing Director Jonathan Metcalf

DK Delhi
Project Editor Neha Ruth Samuel
Senior Art Editor Stuti Tiwari Bhatia
Art Editor Dheeraj Arora
Assistant Editors Nishtha Kapil, Mark Silas
Assistant Art Editor Yamini Panwar
Managing Editors Soma B. Chowdhury, Kingshuk Ghoshal
Managing Art Editor Govind Mittal
Design Consultant Shefali Upadhyay
Senior DTP Designer Tarun Sharma
DTP Designers Anita Yadav, Rakesh Kumar, Harish Aggarwal
Senior Jacket Designer Suhita Dharamjit
Jackets Editorial Coordinator Priyanka Sharma

This American Edition, 2020
First American Edition, 2014
Published in the United States by DK Publishing
1450 Broadway, Suite 801, New York, NY 10018

Copyright © 2014, 2020 Dorling Kindersley Limited
DK, a Division of Penguin Random House LLC
20 21 22 23 24 10 9 8 7 6 5 4 3 2 1
001–322738–May/2020

A catalog record for this book is available from the Library of Congress.
ISBN 978-0-7440-3141-6

DK books are available at special discounts when purchased in bulk for sales promotions, premiums, fund-raising, or educational use. For details, contact: DK Publishing Special Markets, 1450 Broadway, Suite 801, New York, NY 10018
SpecialSales@dk.com

Printed and bound in Canada

All images © Dorling Kindersley Limited
For further information see: www.dkimages.com

For the curious

www.dk.com

Contents

Time Taken

4

Groups of 2

Do not get the blues.
March in 2s.

① Anne has 2 baskets with 5 flowers in each basket.
How many flowers are there in total?
Fill in the numbers.

☐ baskets x ☐ flowers = ☐ flowers

② Complete each sequence:

2   4   6   ☐ ☐ ☐   14   ☐ ☐ ☐   22   ☐

48   46   44   ☐ ☐ ☐ ☐ ☐ ☐ ☐   26

54   56   58   ☐ ☐ ☐ ☐ ☐ ☐ ☐   74   ☐

③ Answer these questions:

Six multiplied by two is   ☐

Seven times two is   ☐

Nine groups of two are   ☐

④ A theater ticket costs $24.50.
How much will 2 tickets cost?

☐

⑤ Solve these multiplication problems:

150	175	236	348	427	519
x 2	x 2	x 2	x 2	x 2	x 2

Time Filler:
Can you recite the 2x table backward?
Time yourself to see how quick you can be.

(6) Divide each number by 2:

76 ⬚   142 ⬚   178 ⬚

(7) Solve these division problems:

⬚   ⬚   ⬚   ⬚   ⬚
2⟌126   2⟌240   2⟌352   2⟌684   2⟌792

(8) Fazir and Tira shared $7.80 equally between them.
How much money did each child receive?

⬚

(9) There were 284 bees in 2 hives. If there was an equal number in each hive, how many bees were there in 1 hive?

⬚ bees

(10) How many shapes are there in each group?

⬚   ⬚

6

Pairs and Doubles

Forget your troubles,
Forget your cares.
Practice doubles and pairs!

(1) Double each number:

25 ☐   42 ☐   70 ☐   127 ☐

(2) How many socks are there in 36 pairs?

☐ socks

(3) In a day, a factory makes wheels for 350 bicycles.
How many wheels are made in 1 day?

☐ wheels

(4) The table below shows some ingredients needed to make 12 cookies.
Calculate how much of each you will need to make 24 cookies.
Hint: Double each amount.

Ingredients	Quantity for 12 Cookies	Quantity for 24 Cookies
Flour	12 oz (350 g)	
Eggs	2	
Butter	8 oz (225 g)	
White sugar	6 oz (175 g)	
Dark chocolate	12 oz (350 g)	
Light brown sugar	6 oz (175 g)	

5 How many wings do 275 crane flies have altogether?
Note: A crane fly has two wings.

[ ] wings

6 The chart shows the number of bunches
of flowers sold in a store in one week.
Write the total for each day.

✿ = 2 bunches

Day	Number of Bunches Sold	Total
Monday	10 x ✿	
Tuesday	8 x ✿	
Wednesday	12 x ✿	
Thursday	9 x ✿	
Friday	20 x ✿	
Saturday	14 x ✿	
Sunday	5 x ✿	

7 Ryan cycles 35 miles, but Jake
cycles twice as far. How far
does Jake cycle?

8 Mom has spent $76.45 on
presents for Jayden, but Dad
has spent double that amount.
How much money has
Dad spent?

Groups of 10

Count up in 10s
Again and again.

1 Tiya had 7 packages. Each package weighed 10 oz.
How much did the packages weigh altogether?

2 Complete these sequences:

10   20   30   ☐ ☐ ☐ ☐ ☐ ☐ ☐

150   140   130   ☐ ☐ ☐ ☐ ☐ ☐ ☐

270   280   290   ☐ ☐ ☐ ☐ ☐ ☐ ☐

3 Answer these questions:

Ten eights are   ☐

Ten times ten is   ☐

Nine multiplied by ten is   ☐

4 Zina saved 35 10-cent coins.
How much money did Zina
have altogether?

5 Solve these multiplication problems:

436	845	152	1,689	791	287
× 10	× 10	× 10	× 10	× 10	× 10

Time Filler:
Think of a 2-digit number. Multiply the number by 10, multiply the same number by 20, and then the same number again by 30. Do you notice a pattern? To multiply your number by 40, try multiplying by 10 then multiplying the answer by 4.

6 Divide each number by 10:

10 ⬚   40 ⬚   80 ⬚   120 ⬚   150 ⬚

7 Solve these division problems:

⬚   ⬚   ⬚   ⬚   ⬚
10)420   10)367   10)780   10)842   10)990

8 How many leaves are there in each group? **Hint:** Multiply the number of rows by the number of columns.

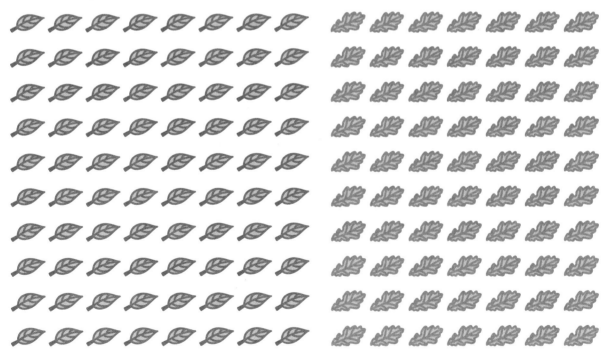

⬚   ⬚

Multiplying by 100 and 1,000

Carefully count the zeroes
To be a math superhero!

(1) Multiply each number by 100:

4 [ ]   47 [ ]   470 [ ]   4,070 [ ]

(2) A box contains 100 T-shirts. How many T-shirts are there in 64 boxes?

[ ] T-shirts

(3) Multiply the number by 100 each time:

3 [ ] [ ] [ ]

82 [ ] [ ] [ ]

(4) How many centimeters are there in 84 m?   [ ]

(5) Divide each number by 100:

42,000 [ ]   702,000 [ ]

804,200 [ ]   6,000,000 [ ]

Time Filler:
What is 30% of $1,500?
Remember: 30% is the same as $\frac{30}{100}$.
So divide $1,500 by 100 and multiply by 30.
It is sale time. Calculate 20% of $80, 40% of $200, and 60% of $45.50.

6) Multiply each number by 1,000:

7 [ ]   82 [ ]   146 [ ]   150 [ ]

7) How many grams are there in 7.2 kg?

[ ]

8) How many cents are there in $35?

[ ]

9) A plane flies at a height of 10,668 m.
What is this height in kilometers?

[ ]

10) A colony of army ants has 700,000 ants. As the ants cross a river, 20% of the colony dies. How many ants make it across?

[ ] ants

Groups of 3

Count in groups of 3.
It is as easy as can be.

1) A jar holds 8 cookies. How many cookies are there in 3 jars?

[   ] cookies

2) Complete each sequence:

0   3   6   [ ] [ ] [ ] [ ] [ ] [ ] [ ]

36   33   30   [ ] [ ] [ ] [ ] [ ] [ ] [ ]

36   39   42   [ ] [ ] [ ] [ ] [ ] [ ] [ ]

3) Answer these questions:

Three fives are [ ]

Three multiplied by seven is [ ]

Three times nine is [ ]

4) Neo bought 6 oranges at 30 ¢ each. What was the total cost of the 6 oranges?

[   ]

5) Solve these multiplication problems:

16	33	55	79	145	229
× 3	× 3	× 3	× 3	× 3	× 3

Time Filler:
Say the 3x table to a rap beat. Singing the times tables helps to learn them. Try saying them to your own musical beats.

(6) Divide each number by 3:

6 ☐   15 ☐   24 ☐   36 ☐   45 ☐

(7) How long will it take Anita to save 42 ¢ if she saves 3 ¢ every week?   ☐ weeks

(8) Solve these division problems:

☐   ☐   ☐   ☐   ☐
3)60   3)90   3)72   3)99   3)183

(9) Pablo was paid $3 for each car that he washed. He earned $39 in one week. How many cars did Pablo wash that week?

☐ cars

(10) How many shapes are there in each group?

☐   ☐

14

Triple Fun

Triple the fun!
Multiply x3 to get these done.

(1) How many wheels are there on 15 tricycles?

[_____] wheels

(2) How many sides do 55 triangles have?

[_____] sides

(3) About 1,800 triplets are born in the United States each year. How many babies is this?

[_____] babies

(4) Thirty-nine trimarans race in a competition. How many hulls are there altogether? **Note:** A trimaran is a boat with 3 hulls.

[_____] hulls

(5) Fifty-four children are split into groups of 3. How many groups of children are there?

[_____] groups

(6) A magnifying glass makes bugs look triple their size. Below are the original sizes of the bugs. What size is each of the bugs when it is magnified?

Worm: 6.5 cm

[_____]

Centipede: 5.25 cm

[_____]

Ladybug: 1.75 cm

[_____]

Time Filler:
How many multiples of 3 are also the answer to other times tables? For example, 12 is a multiple of 3 and is also the answer to 1 x 12, 2 x 6, and 3 x 4. Make a list of all the overlaps.

(7) Packets of cookies are sold in boxes of 3 packets. This chart shows how many boxes are sold from a store in a week. Calculate the number of packets sold that week. = 3 packets

Day	Number of Boxes	Total
Monday		
Tuesday		
Wednesday		
Thursday		
Friday		
Saturday		
Sunday		

(8) Leaving no spaces, fit 9 small triangles (of equal size) inside the large equilateral triangle.

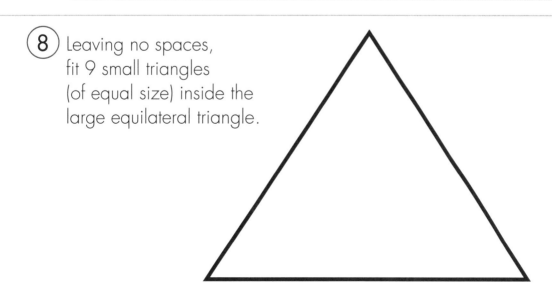

Groups of 4

Are you ready for more?
Here is counting in sets of 4.

1 Share 28 candies equally among 4 children.
How many candies will each child get?

[_____] candies

2 Complete each sequence:

0   4   8

48   44   40

52   56   60

3 Answer these questions:

Nine times four is

Seven groups of four are

Four fives are

4 Dad took Devan, Jesse, and Owen to the fair. The roller coaster ride cost $1.50 for each person. How much did Dad have to pay for all of them to go on the ride?

5 Solve these multiplication problems:

| 23 | 17 | 25 | 115 | 200 | 214 |
| x 4 | x 4 | x 4 | x 4 | x 4 | x 4 |

Time Filler:
Another way to work out the answer to 4 times a number is to multiply the number by 2 and then its answer by 2 again. Choose some numbers between 1 and 20 and give this a try.

(6) Divide each number by 4:

0 ☐   4 ☐   16 ☐   36 ☐   48 ☐

(7) Jeff buys a pack of 4 pencils. The pack costs $1.68. How much does 1 pencil cost?

☐

(8) Solve these division problems:

$4\overline{)56}$ $4\overline{)96}$ $4\overline{)100}$ $4\overline{)128}$ $4\overline{)284}$

(9) A box contains 24 chocolates. They are laid out in 4 equal rows. How many chocolates are there in each row?

☐ chocolates

(10) How many shapes are there in each group?

☐   ☐

Shapes

Count the angles and the sides,
Then read the question and multiply.

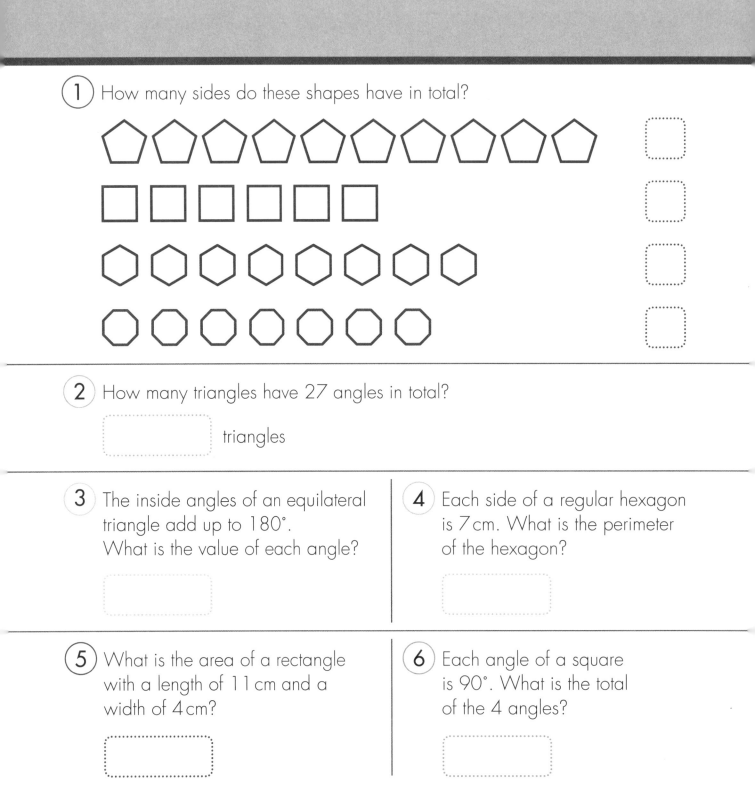

1 How many sides do these shapes have in total?

2 How many triangles have 27 angles in total?

_____ triangles

3 The inside angles of an equilateral triangle add up to 180°.
What is the value of each angle?

4 Each side of a regular hexagon is 7 cm. What is the perimeter of the hexagon?

5 What is the area of a rectangle with a length of 11 cm and a width of 4 cm?

6 Each angle of a square is 90°. What is the total of the 4 angles?

Time Filler:
What times tables will help you solve these problems: What is the perimeter of a regular pentagon with 4-inch-long sides? What is the area of a square with 6-inch-long sides? What is the volume of a cube with 3-inch-long sides?

(7) A rectangular prism has 8 vertices. How many rectangular prisms will have a total of 80 vertices?

rectangular prisms

(8) How many faces do these shapes have?

7 triangular prisms

9 rectangular prisms

12 cylinders

(9) How many edges do these shapes have?

7 cubes

4 square-based pyramids

3 hexagonal prisms

(10) What is the volume of this rectangular prism?
Hint: Volume = length x width x height

6 cm

3 cm

4 cm

Groups of 5

Are you ready to dive
Into counting in 5s?

(1) A pack of greeting cards contains 5 cards.
How many cards are there in 3 packs?

[ ] cards

(2) Complete each sequence:

0	5	10							
60	55	50							
75	80	85							

(3) Answer these questions:

Five groups of six are [ ]

Seven multiplied by five is [ ]

Eleven times five is [ ]

(4) David saved 24 5-cent coins.
How much money did
David save?

[ ]

(5) Solve these multiplication problems:

| 18 | 20 | 49 | 56 | 130 | 222 |
| x 5 | x 5 | x 5 | x 5 | x 5 | x 5 |

Time Filler:
Calculate the total of the following amounts:

- 5 x 10 ¢
- 5 x 5 ¢
- 20 x 5 ¢
- 25 ¢ ÷ 5
- 5 x 25 ¢
- 15 x 5 ¢
- 50 x 5 ¢
- $1 ÷ 5

---

6 Divide each number by 5:

10 ☐   25 ☐   30 ☐   50 ☐   85 ☐

---

7 Five children are given $1.95 to share equally among them. How much money will each child receive?   ☐

---

8 Solve these division problems:

☐   ☐   ☐   ☐   ☐
5)65   5)80   5)125   5)175   5)250

---

9 There are 270 children in a school. There are 5 grades, and each grade has an equal number of children. How many children are there in the 3rd grade?   ☐ children

---

10 How many shapes are there in each group?

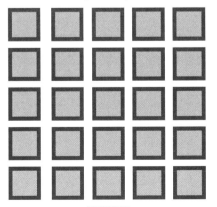

☐   ☐

Telling the Time

Tick tock! Tick tock!
Ready? Then start!

(1) How many minutes are there in 4 hours?

(2) How many minutes is it past 11 o'clock?

(3) How many minutes are there between 9:45 AM and 11:05 AM?

(4) How many minutes are there in 1 day?

(5) How many decades are there in half a century?
   Note: A decade is 10 years; a century is 100 years.

   decades

Time Filler:
If a watch is 5 minutes fast, what is the
actual time if it reads:
9:55? 6:40? 2:20? 3:00?
If a watch is 5 minutes slow, what is the
actual time if it reads:
4:25? 7:00? 11:15? 12:00?

6 How many hours are there in these months?

September (30 days) [ ]   February (28 days) [ ]

May (31 days) [ ]

7 Write the number of minutes past the hour shown on each of these clocks.

[ ]   [ ]   [ ]   [ ]

8 How many minutes are there between 3:10 PM and 5:25 PM?

[ ]

Beat the Clock 1

This is the place to gather pace.
How many answers do you know?
Get ready, get set, and go!

1) $0 \times 3 =$ ☐ 2) $12 \times 2 =$ ☐ 3) $9 \times 5 =$ ☐

4) $1 \times 4 =$ ☐ 5) $11 \times 5 =$ ☐ 6) $3 \times 4 =$ ☐

7) $7 \times 3 =$ ☐ 8) $10 \times 2 =$ ☐ 9) $2 \times 2 =$ ☐

10) $6 \times 5 =$ ☐ 11) $11 \times 4 =$ ☐ 12) $8 \times 2 =$ ☐

13) $4 \times 4 =$ ☐ 14) $10 \times 5 =$ ☐ 15) $2 \times 5 =$ ☐

16) $6 \times 3 =$ ☐ 17) $10 \times 9 =$ ☐ 18) $9 \times 4 =$ ☐

19) $1 \times 5 =$ ☐ 20) $12 \times 4 =$ ☐ 21) $6 \times 4 =$ ☐

22) $7 \times 4 =$ ☐ 23) $10 \times 1 =$ ☐ 24) $12 \times 10 =$ ☐

25) $2 \times 4 =$ ☐ 26) $10 \times 7 =$ ☐ 27) $10 \times 10 =$ ☐

28) $8 \times 4 =$ ☐ 29) $11 \times 2 =$ ☐ 30) $0 \times 2 =$ ☐

Time Filler:
Check your answers on page 80. Return to this page again to improve your score.

31) $24 \div 3 =$ ☐   32) $6 \div 2 =$ ☐   33) $15 \div 5 =$ ☐

34) $30 \div 5 =$ ☐   35) $9 \div 3 =$ ☐   36) $30 \div 10 =$ ☐

37) $14 \div 2 =$ ☐   38) $3 \div 3 =$ ☐   39) $50 \div 10 =$ ☐

40) $40 \div 5 =$ ☐   41) $2 \div 2 =$ ☐   42) $90 \div 10 =$ ☐

43) $21 \div 3 =$ ☐   44) $6 \div 3 =$ ☐   45) $10 \div 10 =$ ☐

46) $18 \div 2 =$ ☐   47) $27 \div 3 =$ ☐   48) $80 \div 10 =$ ☐

49) $15 \div 5 =$ ☐   50) $15 \div 3 =$ ☐   51) $60 \div 10 =$ ☐

52) $40 \div 8 =$ ☐   53) $36 \div 3 =$ ☐   54) $70 \div 10 =$ ☐

55) $18 \div 3 =$ ☐   56) $60 \div 5 =$ ☐   57) $110 \div 10 =$ ☐

58) $30 \div 3 =$ ☐   59) $25 \div 5 =$ ☐   60) $100 \div 10 =$ ☐

Groups of 6

6, 12, 18, 24:
Count in 6s to make numbers more.

1 A tube holds 6 tennis balls. How many balls will 8 tubes hold?

[ ] balls

2 Complete each sequence:

0 6 12 [ ] [ ] [ ] [ ] [ ] [ ] [ ]

72 66 60 [ ] [ ] [ ] [ ] [ ] [ ] [ ]

54 60 66 [ ] [ ] [ ] [ ] [ ] [ ] [ ]

3 Answer these questions:

Six threes are [ ]

Four multiplied by six is [ ]

Six groups of seven are [ ]

4 Selma bought 9 bananas at 6¢ each. How much money did she spend?

[ ]

5 Solve these multiplication problems:

14	25	38	54	116	200
x 6	x 6	x 6	x 6	x 6	x 6

Time Filler:
Another way to work out the answer to 6x a number is to multiply the number by 3 and then double the answer. Choose some numbers between 1 and 20 and give this a try.

6 Divide each number by 6:

18 ☐   30 ☐   66 ☐   72 ☐   96 ☐

7 $2.50 is shared equally among 6 children. How much money is left over?

☐

8 174 cars are parked in 6 rows of equal length. How many cars are there in each row?

☐ cars

9 Solve these division problems:

6⟌90   6⟌102   6⟌204   6⟌276   6⟌348

10 How many items are there in each group?

☐ cabbages   ☐ strawberries

Bugs

Multiply creepy-crawlies' legs
And then count up the butterfly eggs.

① Will recorded the number of bugs he saw in his garden in a month.
How many legs did each type of insect have altogether?
Hint: An insect has 6 legs.

Name of Bug	Number Sighted	Total Number of Legs
Beetle	⊦⊦⊦⊦ ⊦⊦⊦⊦ ⊦⊦⊦⊦ ‖	
Wasp	⊦⊦⊦⊦ ‖‖	
Butterfly	⊦⊦⊦⊦ ⊦⊦⊦⊦ ⊦⊦⊦⊦	
Ladybug	⊦⊦⊦⊦ ⊦⊦⊦⊦ ⊦⊦⊦⊦ ⊦⊦⊦⊦ ‖	

② If a desert locust eats 2 g of food each day, how much will a swarm of 66 million desert locusts eat in a day?

③ A ladybug is about 6 mm long. Under the microscope, the ladybug is magnified 40 times. What size is the ladybug when seen through the microscope?

④ A leaf-cutter ant travels 360 m each day. Altogether, what is the total distance the ant will travel in 60 days?

Time Filler:
A queen honey bee lays 1,500 eggs per day. How many eggs does she lay in 1 month (30 days)? How many eggs does she lay in 6 months (180 days)?

(5) How many wings does a swarm of 6,000 bees have altogether?
Hint: Bees have 4 wings.

[   ] wings

(6) A queen wasp can lay 2,000 eggs a day. How many eggs can she lay in 60 days?

[   ] eggs

(7) A butterfly lays 600 eggs, and only a quarter of them hatch into caterpillars. How many eggs **do not** hatch?

[   ] eggs

(8) Class 5F went to a pond. They made a picture chart of the number of bugs they saw in the pond. How many bugs of each type did they see?

⬤ = 6 bugs   ◗ = 3 bugs

Name of Bug	Number of Bugs	Total
Pond skaters	⬤ ⬤ ⬤ ⬤	
Water bugs	⬤ ⬤ ⬤	
Whirligig beetles	⬤ ⬤ ◗	
Dragonfly nymphs	◗	
Water spiders	⬤	

Sports

Jump, throw, kick, and dash.
You will have this page done in a flash!

(1) Adam ran 400 m in 59 seconds.
Jonas took twice as long.
How long did Jonas take?

(2) Three cyclists raced at 58 mph, 63 mph, and 56 mph. What was their average speed?

(3) These were the results of a season's soccer games:
A win = 5 points, a tie = 3 points, and a loss = 1 point.
How many points did each team get?

Soccer Team	Win	Loss	Tie	Points
United States	8	2	5	
England	7	3	6	
Japan	7	1	7	
Brazil	9	2	4	

(4) The winner of a tennis tournament won
4 times the prize money of a semifinalist.
If a semifinalist received $475,000, how
much money did the winner receive?

Time Filler:
Seven competitors ran a 100 m race in a total time of 91 seconds. What was their average time?

(5) John threw a javelin a distance of 64 m. Amy threw the javelin an eighth ($\frac{1}{8}$) less than John's distance. How far did Amy throw?

(6) Seven race car drivers have a total of 1,645 points. What is the average number of points scored?

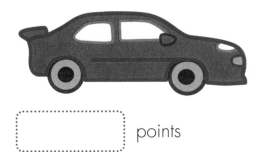

points

(7) There were 162 baseball players taking part in a tournament. . Each team had 9 players. How many teams were there?

teams

(8) The length of a swimming pool is 25 m. This chart shows how many times each child swam that length. How far did each child swim?

Name of Child	Number of Lengths	Total Distance
Harry	10	
Jasmine	8	
Jamie	6	
Heidi	5	

32

Groups of 7

7, 14, 21, 28:
Get started, do not wait!

(1) A dog eats 3 dog treats a day.
How many treats will it eat in 7 days?

[_____] treats

(2) Complete each sequence:

0   7   14   [ ] [ ] [ ] [ ] [ ] [ ] [ ]

84 77 70   [ ] [ ] [ ] [ ] [ ] [ ] [ ]

35 42 49   [ ] [ ] [ ] [ ] [ ] [ ]

(3) Answer these questions:

Seven sixes are [ ]

Eight multiplied by seven is [ ]

Five groups of seven are [ ]

(4) A train ticket costs $7.
How much will 6 tickets cost?

RAILWAYS

[_____]

(5) Solve these multiplication problems:

14	20	35	59	123	246
x 7	x 7	x 7	x 7	x 7	x 7

Time Filler:
Another way to work out or check the answer to 7x a number is to multiply the number by 5, multiply the same number by 2, and then add the two answers. For example: 9 x 7 = (9 x 5) + (9 x 2) = 45 + 18 = 63. Choose a number between 1 and 20 and give this a try.

6 Divide each number by 7:

0 ☐   21 ☐   49 ☐   77 ☐   98 ☐

7 Seven books cost $35.84 altogether. If each book was the same price, what was the price of 1 book?   ☐

8 Solve these division problems:

7)84   7)140   7)105   7)133   7)224

9 Share 42 chairs equally around 7 tables. How many chairs will you keep around each table?   ☐ chairs

10 How many shapes are there in each group?

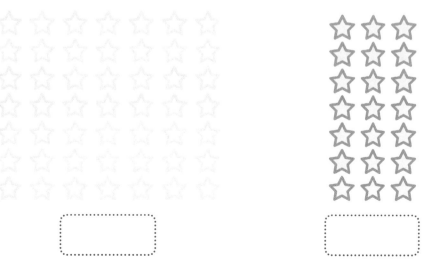

☐   ☐

Days of the Week

Days 7; months 12; weeks 52;
Times tables are fun all year through.

1. How many days are there in 15 weeks?

   [ ] days

2. How many weeks are there in 7 years?
   Note: A year has 52 weeks.

   [ ] weeks

3. How many hours are there in a week?

   [ ]

4. Dad works 35 hours a week. How many hours does he work over 4 weeks?

   [ ]

5. Fran cycles for 30 minutes every day. How many minutes does she cycle in one week?

   [ ]

6. A bookstore opens for 7 hours each day from Monday to Saturday. How many hours is it open in one week?

   BOOKSTORE

   [ ]

Time Filler:
A swimming team exercised 1 hour a day, swam 3 hours a day, and ran 2 hours a day. How many hours did they exercise, swim, and run in 1 week, in 4 weeks, and in 1 year?

(7) Chris practices on the keyboard for 105 minutes every week.
He does an equal amount of time every day.
How long is each practice?

(8) Ella traveled for 91 days. How many weeks is this?

weeks

(9) Dad books a vacation 22 weeks before going.
How many days does the family have to wait?

days

(10) How long in minutes does Kim do these daily activities in one week?

Watching 45 minutes of television

Playing 30 minutes of computer games

Reading for 1 hour 10 minutes

36

Dice and Cards

Playing with dice and cards is fun
When your multiplication work is done.

1 Multiply the two numbers shown on the dice:

6 × 5 = ( )   5 × 4 = ( )

3 × 4 = ( )   1 × 3 = ( )

2 Add the numbers shown on the dice, and then multiply your answer by 6.

{ 1 + 3 } × 6 = ( )   { 1 + 5 } × 6 = ( )

{ 6 + 6 } × 6 = ( )   { 5 + 3 } × 6 = ( )

3 Jack threw a double six 5 times.
What was his total?

( )

4 These are the scores of four players. They each need to throw a double to reach 100 points. What is the number that needs to appear on both dice for each player? Fill in the blanks in the table.

Player	Score	Number Required on Both Dice
1	90	
2	98	
3	94	
4	88	

Time Filler:

Calculate these answers:
- the product of 7 diamonds, 5 diamonds, and 4 diamonds;
- the product of 8 spades, 6 spades, and 2 spades;
- the product of 5 hearts, 9 hearts, and 3 hearts.

⑤ Jess throws a die 100 times and records her scores. What is the total amount scored altogether by Jess? Fill in the blanks in the table.

Number on Die	Number of Times Thrown	Total
1	⊬⊬⊬ ⊬⊬⊬ ⊬⊬⊬ I	
2	⊬⊬⊬ ⊬⊬⊬ ⊬⊬⊬ ⊬⊬⊬	
3	⊬⊬⊬ ⊬⊬⊬ ⊬⊬⊬ III	
4	⊬⊬⊬ ⊬⊬⊬ ⊬⊬⊬	
5	⊬⊬⊬ ⊬⊬⊬ ⊬⊬⊬ II	
6	⊬⊬⊬ ⊬⊬⊬ IIII	
	Total	

⑥ A full deck of cards has 13 cards of each suit.

Note: There are 4 suits in a deck.

How many cards are there in a deck? .... cards

How many cards are there in

4 decks? .... cards

9 decks? .... cards

6 decks? .... cards

Multiply each of these cards by 8:

9 hearts ....

8 diamonds ....

Queen (12) clubs ....

Groups of 8

Get started now and do not be late!
Make steady progress as you count in 8s.

(1) Six trains run every hour. Each train pulls 8 coaches.
How many coaches are pulled every hour?

[ ] coaches

(2) Complete these sequences:

0   8   16   [ ] [ ] [ ] [ ] [ ] [ ] [ ]

96   88   80   [ ] [ ] [ ] [ ] [ ] [ ] [ ]

40   48   56   [ ] [ ] [ ] [ ] [ ] [ ] [ ]

(3) Answer these questions:

Eight sixes are   [ ]

Two multiplied by eight is   [ ]

Nine times eight is   [ ]

(4) A bag of apples costs $1.46.
How much will 8 bags cost?

[ ]

(5) Solve these multiplication problems:

| 15 | 24 | 48 | 97 | 120 | 236 |
| x 8 | x 8 | x 8 | x 8 | x 8 | x 8 |

Time Filler:
Another way to work out the answer to 8x a number is to multiply the number by 4 and then double the answer; or double the number, double the answer, and double again. Choose some numbers between 1 and 20 and give both these ways a try.

6) Solve these division problems:

8)96   8)144   8)168   8)256   8)312

7) Tammy needs 192 m of fencing to go around her garden. Each fencing panel is 8 m long. How many panels will she need?

_____ panels

8) Perry pays $2.80 for 8 pencils. How much did 1 pencil cost?

_____

9) Divide each number by 8:

0 ☐   24 ☐   56 ☐   80 ☐   96 ☐

10) How many gems are there in each group?

Solar System

5, 4, 3, 2, 1;
Blast off into space to get these done.

1. Thirty-five satellites are launched into orbit each year.
   How many satellites have been launched in 8 years?

   [   ] satellites

2. A probe traveling at 500 mph will take 8 years to get to
   Mars. How fast does the probe need to travel to get
   there in 1 year?

   [   ]

3. Mars takes approximately 687 days to orbit the Sun.
   How many days will it take for Mars to orbit the Sun 8 times?

   [   ] days

4. Neptune takes 165 years to orbit the Sun. How many
   years will it take to go around the Sun 8 times?

   [   ] years

5. Mercury takes 88 Earth days to orbit the Sun.
   How many times will Mercury go around the Sun in 880 Earth days?

   [   ] times

Time Filler:
A team of 7 astronauts prepare for an 8-day space mission. If they each need 3.8 lbs of food per day and 2 quarts of water, what is the minimum amount they need to take with them?

(6) Multiply the 8 moons of Neptune with the 16 moons of Jupiter.

|_____| moons

(7) The midday surface temperature of Mercury is 788°F. What is 8 times hotter than the surface of Mercury?

|_____|

(8) Mercury is 4,878 km in diameter. What is an eighth ($\frac{1}{8}$) of its diameter?

|_____|

(9) One day on Saturn lasts 10 hours and 14 minutes on Earth. How long in Earth time will 8 days on Saturn last?

|_____|

One day on Uranus lasts 17 hours and 8 minutes on Earth. How long in Earth time will 8 days on Saturn last?

|_____|

(10) Saturn is 888 million miles away from the Sun. What is $\frac{5}{8}$ of this distance?

|_____|

Jupiter is 484 million miles away from the Sun. What is $\frac{3}{8}$ of this distance?

|_____|

Fractions

Split the whole by the denominator,
Then multiply by the numerator.

① What is half ($\frac{1}{2}$) of each number?

18 ☐   10 ☐   6 ☐   24 ☐

② What is a third ($\frac{1}{3}$) of each amount?

12 g ☐   27 g ☐   33 g ☐   42 g ☐

③ What is a quarter ($\frac{1}{4}$) of each number?

4 ☐   20 ☐   36 ☐   52 ☐

④ There are 60 carrots in a box.
How many carrots make up…

$\frac{7}{10}$ of the box? ☐ carrots

$\frac{1}{10}$ of the box? ☐ carrots $\frac{2}{10}$ of the box? ☐ carrots

⑤ There were 25 bananas, and $\frac{1}{5}$ were eaten.
How many bananas are left?

☐ bananas

Time Filler:

Calculate the following amounts:

$\frac{5}{9}$ of 450 oz; $\frac{7}{10}$ of $2.50; $\frac{3}{8}$ of 640 in.

Write some fraction challenges for your friends. Did they get them right?

---

6 What is three quarters ($\frac{3}{4}$) of each number?

12 [ ]   24 [ ]   32 [ ]   44 [ ]

---

7 What is $\frac{1}{8}$ of 48 slices of pizza?

[ ] slices

---

8 What is $\frac{7}{10}$ of 40?

[ ]

---

9 There are 30 children in a class. $\frac{3}{5}$ of the class have lunch in the cafeteria. How many children **do not** have lunch in the cafeteria?

[ ] children

---

10 Oliver picked 54 apples. $\frac{1}{6}$ were rotten. How many apples were rotten?

[ ] apples

Groups of 9

Wide awake and ready to shine?
Here is counting in sets of nine.

(1) There are 8 horse races in a day. If 9 different horses took part in each race, how many horses ran that day?

[   ] horses

(2) Complete each sequence:

0   9   18   [ ] [ ] [ ] [ ] [ ] [ ] [ ]

108   99   90   [ ] [ ] [ ] [ ] [ ] [ ] [ ]

45   54   63   [ ] [ ] [ ] [ ] [ ] [ ] [ ]

(3) Answer these questions:

Three multiplied by nine is   [ ]

Nine eights are   [ ]

Six groups of nine are   [ ]

(4) A bunch of flowers costs $4.99. How much will 9 bunches cost?

[   ]

(5) Solve these multiplication problems:

16	23	92	47	150	218
x 9	x 9	x 9	x 9	x 9	x 9

Time Filler:
Another way to work out the answer to 9x a number is to multiply the number by 10 and then take away the number from the answer. For example, 15 x 9 = (15 x 10) − 15 = 135. Choose some 2-digit numbers and give this a try.

6 Divide each number by 9:

9 ⬚   36 ⬚   45 ⬚   90 ⬚   108 ⬚

7 Jake needed $468 to buy a new television. He decided to save an equal amount over 9 weeks to reach the total. What is the amount he needed to save each week?

8 How many shapes are there in each group?

Shopping

Pick, choose, and weigh;
Then go to the checkout to pay!

① Calculate the total cost that Karl spent shopping.

Item	Cost per item	Amount	Total
Tomatoes	20 ¢	6	
Carrots	10 ¢	8	
Cabbage	89 ¢	2	
Peppers	43 ¢	5	
Cheese	$1.26	1	
Bread	76 ¢	3	
Juice	$1.49	4	
Milk	72 ¢	6	
Cookies	89 ¢	7	
Pasta	$2.56	2	

Time Filler:
Calculate the total of these amounts:
- 3 pounds of apples at 45 ¢ a pound;
- 7 oranges at 23 ¢ each;
- 6 cans of soup at $1.20 a can.
  Which is cheaper?
  12 packets of cookies at 54 ¢ each
  or 9 jars of jam at 63 ¢ each?

(2) A storekeeper sold 6 red coats at $89 each.
How much did the red coats cost altogether?

(3) Mom bought 3 bracelets at $7.84 each.
How much money did Mom spend?

(4) Tami spent $77.97 on 3 pairs of shoes. Each pair cost the same
amount. How much did each pair cost?

(5) In a sale, the cost of a hat was reduced by 20%. The original price
of the hat was $14.50. How much was it reduced by?

48

Beat the Clock 2

This is the place to gather pace.
How many answers do you know?
Get ready, get set, and go!

1) 0 x 9 =

2) 0 x 6 =

3) 8 x 9 =

4) 5 x 8 =

5) 7 x 8 =

6) 3 x 8 =

7) 2 x 9 =

8) 7 x 6 =

9) 2 x 7 =

10) 1 x 7 =

11) 9 x 9 =

12) 10 x 9 =

13) 2 x 8 =

14) 1 x 8 =

15) 12 x 6 =

16) 3 x 6 =

17) 9 x 7 =

18) 10 x 7 =

19) 4 x 7 =

20) 4 x 9 =

21) 11 x 6 =

22) 8 x 8 =

23) 6 x 8 =

24) 11 x 8 =

25) 9 x 6 =

26) 6 x 7 =

27) 12 x 7 =

28) 5 x 6 =

29) 7 x 7 =

30) 12 x 9 =

Time Filler:
Check your answers on page 80. Return to this page again to improve your score.

(31) $0 \div 7 =$ ☐ (32) $60 \div 6 =$ ☐ (33) $63 \div 9 =$ ☐

(34) $0 \div 8 =$ ☐ (35) $99 \div 9 =$ ☐ (36) $84 \div 7 =$ ☐

(37) $9 \div 9 =$ ☐ (38) $27 \div 9 =$ ☐ (39) $48 \div 8 =$ ☐

(40) $6 \div 6 =$ ☐ (41) $96 \div 8 =$ ☐ (42) $72 \div 8 =$ ☐

(43) $21 \div 7 =$ ☐ (44) $32 \div 8 =$ ☐ (45) $63 \div 7 =$ ☐

(46) $24 \div 6 =$ ☐ (47) $45 \div 9 =$ ☐ (48) $35 \div 7 =$ ☐

(49) $77 \div 7 =$ ☐ (50) $48 \div 6 =$ ☐ (51) $54 \div 9 =$ ☐

(52) $80 \div 8 =$ ☐ (53) $49 \div 7 =$ ☐ (54) $12 \div 6 =$ ☐

(55) $36 \div 6 =$ ☐ (56) $64 \div 8 =$ ☐ (57) $56 \div 7 =$ ☐

(58) $40 \div 8 =$ ☐ (59) $81 \div 9 =$ ☐ (60) $108 \div 9 =$ ☐

Division

Use your times tables know-how
To work out division questions now.

(1) Match each question to its answer:

168 ÷ 6   524 ÷ 4   595 ÷ 7   729 ÷ 9

85   81   28   131

(2) Use the long division method to solve each problem:

4) 648   2) 496   5) 760   6) 822

(3) What is the remainder each time?

592 ÷ 3 □   264 ÷ 7 □

786 ÷ 4 □   543 ÷ 9 □

(4) Circle all the multiples of 7:

14   23   35   43   76   84

Time Filler:
How many multiples of 9 are also the answer to other times tables? For example, 18 is a multiple of 9 and is also the answer to 1 x 18, 2 x 9, and 3 x 6. Make a list of all the overlaps.

---

5 Circle all the multiples of 9:

28   54   61   83   99   108

---

6 Circle all the multiples of 12:

24   45   60   56   72   98   132

---

7 Solve these money problems:

$14.58 ÷ 3 = [   ] $35.60 ÷ 8 = [   ]

$26.96 ÷ 4 = [   ] $66.69 ÷ 9 = [   ]

---

8 List all the factors for each number:

24   ▢ ▢ ▢ ▢ ▢ ▢ ▢ ▢

36   ▢ ▢ ▢ ▢ ▢ ▢ ▢ ▢ ▢

72   ▢ ▢ ▢ ▢ ▢ ▢ ▢ ▢ ▢ ▢ ▢ ▢

100 ▢ ▢ ▢ ▢ ▢ ▢ ▢ ▢ ▢

Groups of 11

11, 22, 33, 44;
Follow the pattern to find more.

① A farmer plants 6 rows of tulips, with 11 bulbs in each row.
How many tulip bulbs are planted?

[   ] bulbs

② Complete each sequence:

0   11   22   [   ] [   ] [   ] [   ] [   ] [   ] [   ]

143   132   121   [   ] [   ] [   ] [   ] [   ] [   ]

66   77   88   [   ] [   ] [   ] [   ] [   ] [   ] [   ]

③ Answer these questions:

Eleven fours are [   ]

Eleven groups of seven are [   ]

Twelve times eleven is [   ]

④ Ellie buys 11 T-shirts at $1.10
each. How much does Ellie
pay for 11 T-shirts?

[   ]

⑤ Solve these multiplication problems:

14	25	69	33	81	100
× 11	× 11	× 11	× 11	× 11	× 11

Time Filler:
Another way to work out or check the answer to 11x a number is to multiply the number by 10 and then add on the number to the answer. For example, 23 x 11 = (23 x 10) + 23 = 253. Choose some 2-digit numbers and give this a try.

6) Divide each number by 11:

22 ☐   88 ☐   121 ☐   143 ☐   176 ☐

7) Solve these division problems:

11)187   11)297   11)363   11)572   11)781

8) How many spots are there in each group?

54

Buildings

Count the windows, stairs, and doors;
Multiply them by the number of floors.

① Each stairway of an apartment building has 12 steps.
How many steps are there in 6 stairways?

[   ] steps

② A window cleaner takes 1 hour to clean 20 windows.
How long will it take him to clean 120 windows?

[   ]

③ There are 210 windows in a 7-story office building. There
is an equal number of windows on each story. How many
windows are there on the fifth story?

[   ] windows

④ An apartment building has 15 stories and 6 apartments on
each story. How many apartments are there altogether?

[   ] apartments

⑤ A school has 4 hallways with
9 classrooms in each hallway. How
many classrooms are there altogether?

[   ] classrooms

Time Filler:
If a 72-story skyscraper has 100 windows, 63 offices, and 7 meeting rooms on each story, how many windows, offices, and meeting rooms are there in total?

6) A builder uses 500 tiles to cover half a roof of a house. How many tiles will he need for 6 houses?

[ ] tiles

7) A 10-story hotel has a total of 378 rooms. The rooms are on floors 2 to 10. If there is an equal number of rooms on each floor, how many rooms are there on the eighth floor?

[ ] rooms

8) A house costs $285,000. The real estate agent receives 5% of the sale price. How much money does the agent receive?

[ ]

9) Two-thirds ($\frac{2}{3}$) of the 126 houses on Grove Avenue have garages. How many houses **do not** have garages?

[ ] houses

10) A store has an area of $620\,m^2$. If the width of the store is 20 m, what is its length?

[ ]

Sequences

Find the number pattern for each row;
The times tables facts are fun to know.

(1) Fill in the missing numbers in each sequence:

5   10   ☐   ☐   ☐   30   ☐   ☐   45   ☐

60   ☐   ☐   75   ☐   ☐   ☐   95   ☐   105

(2) Complete each sequence:

4   8   12   ☐   ☐   ☐   ☐   ☐   ☐   ☐

7   14   21   ☐   ☐   ☐   ☐   ☐   ☐   ☐

25   50   75   ☐   ☐   ☐   ☐   ☐   ☐   ☐

(3) Continue this pattern:

(4) Complete this chart:

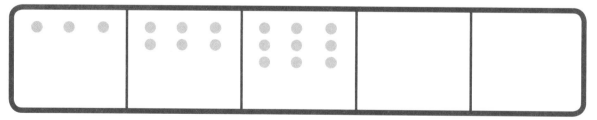

×	0	1	2	3	4	5	6	7	8	9	10
6											
9											

Time Filler:
Can you work out the numbers
in these sequences:
- start on 3 and multiply by 3 for 6 steps?
- start on 8 and double the number for
  5 steps?

(5) Fill in the missing numbers in each sequence:

80   72   [ ] [ ] [ ]   40   [ ] [ ] [ ]   8

60   56   52   [ ] [ ] [ ]   36   [ ] [ ] [ ]

(6) Continue this pattern:

(7) Complete this chart:

x	10	9	8	7	6	5	4	3	2	1	0
11											
12											

(8) Complete each sequence:

200   190   180   [ ] [ ] [ ] [ ] [ ] [ ]

150   148   146   [ ] [ ] [ ] [ ] [ ] [ ]

58

Groups of 12

Here is the last of the times tables;
You know most of these.
They have been in the others,
So you can answer with ease.

① A baker takes an hour to cook 12 loaves of bread.
How many loaves can he make in 3 hours?

[ ] loaves

② Complete each sequence:

0 12 24 [ ] [ ] [ ] [ ] [ ] [ ] [ ]

144 132 120 [ ] [ ] [ ] [ ] [ ] [ ] [ ]

60 72 84 [ ] [ ] [ ] [ ] [ ] [ ]

③ Answer these questions:

Five groups of twelve are [ ]

Eight times twelve is [ ]

Ten multiplied by twelve is [ ]

④ Cara collects trading cards. She buys 12 packs of 4 cards at $2 per pack. How much money does Cara spend and how many trading cards will she have?

[ ] [ ] trading cards

⑤ Solve these multiplication problems.

13	17	24	35	42	100
x 12	x 12	x 12	x 12	x 12	x 12

Time Filler:
Another way to work out or check the answer to 12x a number is to multiply the number by 10, multiply the number by 2, and then add the two answers. For example: 14 x 12 = (14 x 10) + (14 x 2) = 140 + 28 = 168. Choose some 2-digit numbers and give this a try.

6 Divide each number by 12:

0 ⬚   48 ⬚   84 ⬚   132 ⬚   192 ⬚

7 Mom has a loan of $864, which she pays back in equal amounts over 12 months. How much does Mom pay each month?

8 How many shapes are there in each group?

Dozen a Day

Keep multiplying by 12 to find the way
To get the answers for a Dozen a Day.

(1) A dozen children split themselves equally into 3 teams to play a game.
How many children are there in each team?

.... children

(2) Cupcakes were sold in boxes of 12.
How many cupcakes were there in 15 boxes?

.... cupcakes

(3) How many dozen eggs are there in
a gross of eggs? **Hint:** A gross is 144.

....

(4) What are the factors of 12?

☐ ☐ ☐ ☐ ☐ ☐

(5) A score of children had 12 candies each.
How many candies did they have altogether?
Note: A score is 20.

.... candies

Time Filler:
How many cartons of a dozen eggs will be needed to pack 216 eggs? 300 eggs? 432 eggs? How many eggs are there in 42 cartons, each with a dozen eggs?

6 A chef cooks a batch of 12 pancakes in 12 minutes. How many batches of 12 pancakes can he make in an hour?

.... batches

7 Trains arrived at Whistlestop Station 3 times an hour. How many trains arrived in 12 hours?

.... trains

8 A group of musicians performed a dozen pieces in a concert. Each piece lasted 4 minutes. How many minutes did the musicians perform altogether?

....

9 900 raffle tickets were sold at a fund-raising event. There were a dozen prizes. What was the chance of winning a prize? Circle the correct answer.

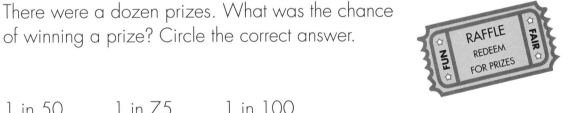

1 in 50   1 in 75   1 in 100

10 Once a month, Jill ran a distance of 5,000 meters in a cross-country event. How many meters did Jill run in a year?

Plants

Flowers, fruits, vegetables, and trees;
If you know your times tables,
You will answer these with ease.

1) A bee visits 47 flowers each trip before returning
to its hive. How many flowers will it visit in 5 trips?

[　　　　] flowers

2) A tulip has 6 petals. How many petals will
24 tulips have altogether?

[　　　　] petals

3) A flower arranger used 112 poppies for her arrangement.
Half were red, $\frac{3}{8}$ were yellow, and the rest were orange.
How many poppies of each color did the flower arranger use?

[　　　　] red   [　　　　] yellow   [　　　　] orange

4) A gardener plants 5 rows with 14 potatoes in each row.
How many potato plants does that make altogether?

[　　　　] plants

5) Jim plants 2 bean seeds in each flower pot. He has 38 seeds
in a packet. How many flower pots will Jim need?

[　　　　] pots

Time Filler:
A gardener is planning his square garden.
Calculate how many of each plant he needs:
- 4 rows of 8 fruit trees in each row;
- 7 shrubs for each side;
- 6 V-shaped rows of 12 flowers for each row;
- 5 plant pots with a tepee of 3 climbing plants in each.

(6) A farmer grows 64 cabbages in each row.
How many cabbages does he grow in 12 rows?

    [_____] cabbages

(7) Nina's pumpkin weighs 22 kg, but Peter's pumpkin weighs 3 times as much. How much does Peter's pumpkin weigh?

    [_____]

(8) Vinny picks 340 apples. He puts an equal number into each of 4 crates. How many apples are there in 1 crate?

    [_____] apples

(9) A tree seedling grows 60 cm a year. How tall will it be after 18 years?

    [_____]

(10) A pine tree is $\frac{1}{5}$ the height of a giant redwood tree, which is 115 m tall.
What is the height of the pine tree?

    [_____]

Beat the Clock 3

This is the place to gather pace.
How many answers do you know?
Get ready, get set, and go!

1) 3 x 9 = ☐ 2) 19 x 4 = ☐ 3) 20 x 6 = ☐

4) 1 x 7 = ☐ 5) 12 x 9 = ☐ 6) 12 x 8 = ☐

7) 4 x 6 = ☐ 8) 10 x 8 = ☐ 9) 12 x 5 = ☐

10) 5 x 4 = ☐ 11) 11 x 0 = ☐ 12) 11 x 2 = ☐

13) 5 x 8 = ☐ 14) 11 x 6 = ☐ 15) 18 x 3 = ☐

16) 8 x 2 = ☐ 17) 12 x 4 = ☐ 18) 16 x 2 = ☐

19) 7 x 7 = ☐ 20) 10 x 5 = ☐ 21) 14 x 0 = ☐

22) 7 x 3 = ☐ 23) 15 x 9 = ☐ 24) 32 x 1 = ☐

25) 1 x 3 = ☐ 26) 17 x 8 = ☐ 27) 19 x 10 = ☐

28) 2 x 10 = ☐ 29) 15 x 7 = ☐ 30) 16 x 12 = ☐

Time Filler:
Check your answers on page 80. Return to this page again to improve your score.

(31) $54 \div 9 =$ ☐   (32) $245 \div 5 =$ ☐   (33) $85 \div 5 =$ ☐

(34) $81 \div 9 =$ ☐   (35) $112 \div 8 =$ ☐   (36) $24 \div 3 =$ ☐

(37) $56 \div 8 =$ ☐   (38) $100 \div 5 =$ ☐   (39) $92 \div 2 =$ ☐

(40) $56 \div 7 =$ ☐   (41) $108 \div 6 =$ ☐   (42) $63 \div 3 =$ ☐

(43) $42 \div 6 =$ ☐   (44) $456 \div 1 =$ ☐   (45) $28 \div 2 =$ ☐

(46) $91 \div 7 =$ ☐   (47) $537 \div 3 =$ ☐   (48) $76 \div 2 =$ ☐

(49) $40 \div 4 =$ ☐   (50) $860 \div 10 =$ ☐   (51) $99 \div 11 =$ ☐

(52) $25 \div 5 =$ ☐   (53) $240 \div 12 =$ ☐   (54) $320 \div 10 =$ ☐

(55) $51 \div 3 =$ ☐   (56) $143 \div 11 =$ ☐   (57) $144 \div 12 =$ ☐

(58) $64 \div 4 =$ ☐   (59) $121 \div 11 =$ ☐   (60) $1,000 \div 10 =$ ☐

Answers:

4–5 Groups of 2
6–7 Pairs and Doubles

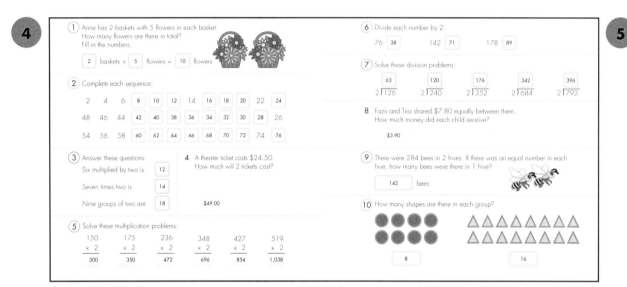

4

1. Anne has 2 baskets with 5 flowers in each basket. How many flowers are there in total? Fill in the numbers.

   2 baskets × 5 flowers = 10 flowers

2. Complete each sequence:

   2 4 6 **8** **10** **12** 14 **16** 18 20 22 **24**

   48 46 44 **42** **40** **38** 34 **32** 30 28 **26**

   54 56 58 **60** **62** **64** 66 68 70 72 74 76

3. Answer these questions:
   Six multiplied by two is **12**
   Seven times two is **14**
   Nine groups of two are **18**

4. A theater ticket costs $24.50. How much will 2 tickets cost?

   $49.00

5. Solve these multiplication problems:

150	175	236	348	427	519
× 2	× 2	× 2	× 2	× 2	× 2
300	**350**	**472**	**696**	**854**	**1,038**

5

6. Divide each number by 2:

   76 **38**   142 **71**   178 **89**

7. Solve these division problems:

63	**120**	**176**	**342**	**396**
2) 126	2) 240	2) 352	2) 684	2) 792

8. Fazir and Tira shared $7.80 equally between them. How much money did each child receive?

   $3.90

9. There were 284 bees in 2 hives. If there was an equal number in each hive, how many bees were there in 1 hive?

   142 bees

10. How many shapes are there in each group?

    8   **16**

All the pages in this book are intended for children who are familiar with the 0 to 12 times tables and are able to solve long multiplication and division problems. At this age, your child will know that multiplication is a fast way of adding equal groups of numbers.

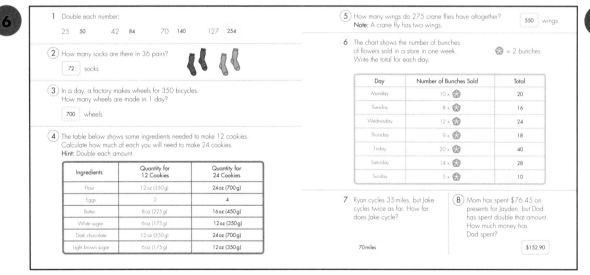

6

1. Double each number:

   25 **50**   42 **84**   70 **140**   127 **254**

2. How many socks are there in 36 pairs?

   72 socks

3. In a day, a factory makes wheels for 350 bicycles. How many wheels are made in 1 day?

   700 wheels

4. The table below shows some ingredients needed to make 12 cookies. Calculate how much of each you will need to make 24 cookies.
   Hint: Double each amount.

Ingredients	Quantity for 12 Cookies	Quantity for 24 Cookies
Flour	12 oz (350 g)	24 oz (700 g)
Eggs	2	4
Butter	8 oz (225 g)	16 oz (450 g)
White sugar	6 oz (175 g)	12 oz (350 g)
Dark chocolate	12 oz (350 g)	24 oz (700 g)
Light brown sugar	6 oz (175 g)	12 oz (350 g)

7

5. How many wings do 275 crane flies have altogether?   **550** wings
   Note: A crane fly has two wings.

6. The chart shows the number of bunches of flowers sold in a store in one week. Write the total for each day.   ⭐ = 2 bunches

Day	Number of Bunches Sold	Total
Monday	10 × ⭐	20
Tuesday	8 × ⭐	16
Wednesday	12 × ⭐	24
Thursday	9 × ⭐	18
Friday	20 × ⭐	40
Saturday	14 × ⭐	28
Sunday	5 × ⭐	10

7. Ryan cycles 35 miles, but Jake cycles twice as far. How far does Jake cycle?

   70 miles

8. Mom has spent $76.45 on presents for Jayden, but Dad has spent double that amount. How much money has Dad spent?

   $152.90

Children will be ready for challenging questions to apply their times tables knowledge. They will learn to read the question carefully, identify the data, and decide which of the four operations to use, which will be either to multiply or to divide in this book.

Answers:

8–9 Groups of 10
10–11 Multiplying by 100 and 1,000

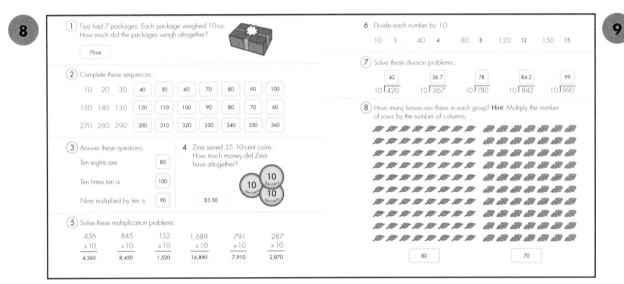

8

① Tiya had 7 packages. Each package weighed 10oz. How much did the packages weigh altogether?

70oz

② Complete these sequences:

| 10 | 20 | 30 | 40 | 50 | 60 | 70 | 80 | 90 | 100 |

| 150 | 140 | 130 | 120 | 110 | 100 | 90 | 80 | 70 | 60 |

| 270 | 280 | 290 | 300 | 310 | 320 | 330 | 340 | 350 | 360 |

③ Answer these questions:

Ten eights are — 80

Ten times ten is — 100

Nine multiplied by ten is — 90

4 Zina saved 35 10-cent coins. How much money did Zina have altogether?

$3.50

⑤ Solve these multiplication problems:

436	845	152	1,689	791	287
×10	×10	×10	×10	×10	×10
4,360	8,450	1,520	16,890	7,910	2,870

9

6 Divide each number by 10:

| 10 | 1 | 40 | 4 | 80 | 8 | 120 | 12 | 150 | 15 |

⑦ Solve these division problems:

| 42 | 36.7 | 78 | 84.2 | 99 |
| 10)420 | 10)367 | 10)780 | 10)842 | 10)990 |

⑧ How many leaves are there in each group? **Hint:** Multiply the number of rows by the number of columns.

80   70

Children will know that multiplying by 10 means to make amounts ten times bigger. In the case of decimals, this means moving the decimal point one place to the right to multiply and moving the decimal point one place to the left to divide.

10

① Multiply each number by 100:

| 4 | 400 | 47 | 4,700 | 470 | 47,000 | 4,070 | 407,000 |

② A box contains 100 T-shirts. How many T-shirts are there in 64 boxes?

6,400 T-shirts

3 Multiply the number by 100 each time:

| 3 | 300 | 30,000 | 3,000,000 |
| 82 | 8,200 | 820,000 | 82,000,000 |

④ How many centimeters are there in 84m?

8,400cm

⑤ Divide each number by 100:

| 42,000 | 420 | | 702,000 | 7,020 |
| 804,200 | 8,042 | | 6,000,000 | 60,000 |

11

⑥ Multiply each number by 1,000:

| 7 | 7,000 | 82 | 82,000 | 146 | 146,000 | 150 | 150,000 |

⑦ How many grams are there in 7.2kg?

7,200g

⑧ How many cents are there in $35?

3,500¢

⑨ A plane flies at a height of 10,668m. What is this height in kilometers?

10.668km

⑩ A colony of army ants has 700,000 ants. As the ants cross a river, 20% of the colony dies. How many ants make it across?

560,000 ants

Children will be familiar with the equivalents between metric units of measurement and that metric is based on multiples of 10. Some of these questions require the knowledge that 100cm = 1m, 1,000m = 1km, and 1,000g = 1kg. Also, dividing by 100 helps solve percentage problems, as *percent* means part per 100.

Answers:

12–13 Groups of 3
14–15 Triple Fun

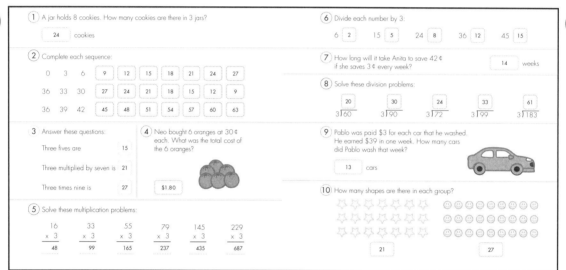

12

1 A jar holds 8 cookies. How many cookies are there in 3 jars?

24 cookies

2 Complete each sequence:

0	3	6	9	12	15	18	21	24	27
36	33	30	27	24	21	18	15	12	9
36	39	42	45	48	51	54	57	60	63

3 Answer these questions:

Three fives are — 15

Three multiplied by seven is — 21

Three times nine is — 27

4 Neo bought 6 oranges at 30 ¢ each. What was the total cost of the 6 oranges?

$1.80

5 Solve these multiplication problems:

16	33	55	79	145	229
× 3	× 3	× 3	× 3	× 3	× 3
48	99	165	237	435	687

13

6 Divide each number by 3:

6 — 2   15 — 5   24 — 8   36 — 12   45 — 15

7 How long will it take Anita to save 42 ¢ if she saves 3 ¢ every week?

14 weeks

8 Solve these division problems:

20 ÷ 3|60   30 ÷ 3|90   24 ÷ 3|72   33 ÷ 3|99   61 ÷ 3|183

9 Pablo was paid $3 for each car that he washed. He earned $39 in one week. How many cars did Pablo wash that week?

13 cars

10 How many shapes are there in each group?

21   27

These orange pages focus on a particular times table and provide a wide range of questions to reinforce your child's familiarity with the specific times table. The sequences support their knowledge of the multiples, which is very useful to know when solving division problems.

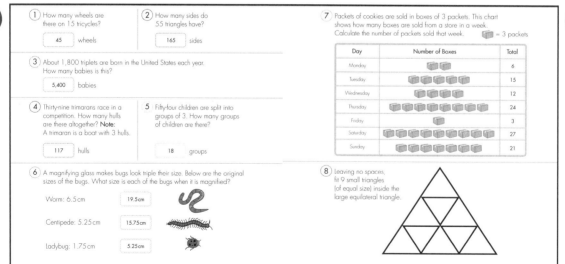

14

1 How many wheels are there on 15 tricycles?

45 wheels

2 How many sides do 55 triangles have?

165 sides

3 About 1,800 triplets are born in the United States each year. How many babies is this?

5,400 babies

4 Thirty-nine trimarans race in a competition. How many hulls are there altogether? **Note:** A trimaran is a boat with 3 hulls.

117 hulls

5 Fifty-four children are split into groups of 3. How many groups of children are there?

18 groups

6 A magnifying glass makes bugs look triple their size. Below are the original sizes of the bugs. What size is each of the bugs when it is magnified?

Worm: 6.5 cm — 19.5 cm

Centipede: 5.25 cm — 15.75 cm

Ladybug: 1.75 cm — 5.25 cm

15

7 Packets of cookies are sold in boxes of 3 packets. This chart shows how many boxes are sold from a store in a week. Calculate the number of packets sold that week. = 3 packets

Day	Number of Boxes	Total
Monday		6
Tuesday		15
Wednesday		12
Thursday		24
Friday		3
Saturday		27
Sunday		21

8 Leaving no spaces, fit 9 small triangles (of equal size) inside the large equilateral triangle.

These red pages are themed and based on a particular times table. Times table knowledge is relevant and can be useful in many everyday activities and situations. Hopefully, children can be motivated and will understand that multiplication and division facts are applicable to life.

Answers:

16–17 Groups of 4
18–19 Shapes

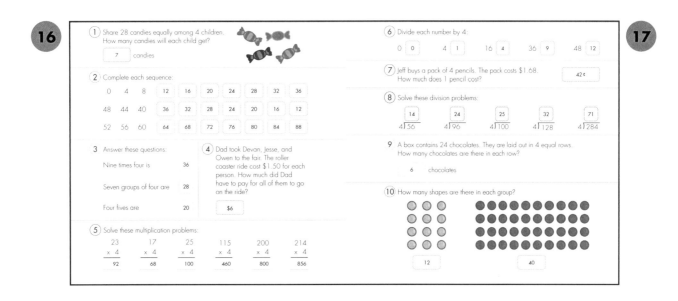

16

1. Share 28 candies equally among 4 children. How many candies will each child get?
   7 candies

2. Complete each sequence:

0	4	8	12	16	20	24	28	32	36
48	44	40	36	32	28	24	20	16	12
52	56	60	64	68	72	76	80	84	88

3. Answer these questions:
   Nine times four is   36
   Seven groups of four are   28
   Four fives are   20

4. Dad took Devan, Jesse, and Owen to the fair. The roller coaster ride cost $1.50 for each person. How much did Dad have to pay for all of them to go on the ride?
   $6

5. Solve these multiplication problems:

23	17	25	115	200	214
× 4	× 4	× 4	× 4	× 4	× 4
92	68	100	460	800	856

17

6. Divide each number by 4:
   0 **0**   4 **1**   16 **4**   36 **9**   48 **12**

7. Jeff buys a pack of 4 pencils. The pack costs $1.68. How much does 1 pencil cost?
   42¢

8. Solve these division problems:
   14 4⟌56   **24** 4⟌96   **25** 4⟌100   **32** 4⟌128   **71** 4⟌284

9. A box contains 24 chocolates. They are laid out in 4 equal rows. How many chocolates are there in each row?
   6   chocolates

10. How many shapes are there in each group?
    12   40

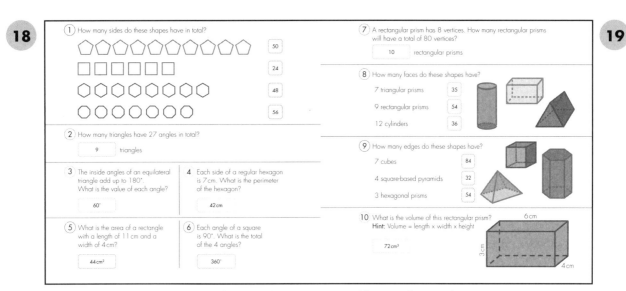

18

1. How many sides do these shapes have in total?
   50
   24
   48
   56

2. How many triangles have 27 angles in total?
   9 triangles

3. The inside angles of an equilateral triangle add up to 180°. What is the value of each angle?
   60°

4. Each side of a regular hexagon is 7 cm. What is the perimeter of the hexagon?
   42 cm

5. What is the area of a rectangle with a length of 11 cm and a width of 4 cm?
   44 cm²

6. Each angle of a square is 90°. What is the total of the 4 angles?
   360°

19

7. A rectangular prism has 8 vertices. How many rectangular prisms will have a total of 80 vertices?
   10   rectangular prisms

8. How many faces do these shapes have?
   7 triangular prisms   35
   9 rectangular prisms   54
   12 cylinders   36

9. How many edges do these shapes have?
   7 cubes   84
   4 square-based pyramids   32
   3 hexagonal prisms   54

10. What is the volume of this rectangular prism?
    Hint: Volume = length × width × height
    72 cm³   6 cm   3 cm   4 cm

On these green pages, knowledge of times tables is applied to a general Math concept. Shapes offer many opportunities for multiplying and dividing problems, such as working out perimeters, areas, and volumes.

Answers:

20–21 Groups of 5
22–23 Telling the Time

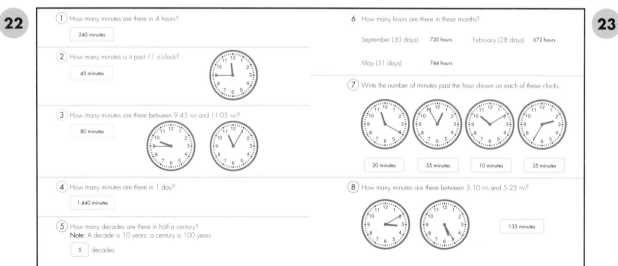

20

1. A pack of greeting cards contains 5 cards. How many cards are there in 3 packs?

   15 cards

2. Complete each sequence:

   0 5 10 **15 20 25 30 35 40 45**

   60 55 50 **45 40 35 30 25 20 15**

   75 80 85 **90 95 100 105 110 115 120**

3. Answer these questions:

   Five groups of six are **30**

   Seven multiplied by five is **35**

   Eleven times five is **55**

4. David saved 24 5-cent coins. How much money did David save?

   $1.20

5. Solve these multiplication problems:

18	20	49	56	130	222
× 5	× 5	× 5	× 5	× 5	× 5
90	**100**	**245**	**280**	**650**	**1,110**

21

6. Divide each number by 5:

   10 **2**   25 **5**   30 **6**   50 **10**   85 **17**

7. Five children are given $1.95 to share equally among them. How much money will each child receive?

   39¢

8. Solve these division problems:

   13 5)65   **16** 5)80   **25** 5)125   **35** 5)175   **50** 5)250

9. There are 270 children in a school. There are 5 grades, and each grade has an equal number of children. How many children are there in the 3rd grade?

   54 children

10. How many shapes are there in each group?

    25   **40**

22

1. How many minutes are there in 4 hours?

   240 minutes

2. How many minutes is it past 11 o'clock?

   45 minutes

3. How many minutes are there between 9:45 AM and 11:05 AM?

   80 minutes

4. How many minutes are there in 1 day?

   1,440 minutes

5. How many decades are there in half a century?
   Note: A decade is 10 years; a century is 100 years.

   5 decades

23

6. How many hours are there in these months?

   September (30 days) **720 hours**   February (28 days) **672 hours**

   May (31 days) **744 hours**

7. Write the number of minutes past the hour shown on each of these clocks.

   20 minutes   **55 minutes**   **10 minutes**   **35 minutes**

8. How many minutes are there between 3:10 PM and 5:25 PM?

   135 minutes

Telling time and calculating the duration of time passing involves working with multiples of the five times table on occasion. The position of the minute hand can be quickly worked out by multiplying the numbers on a clock by five.

Answers:

26–27 Groups of 6
28–29 Bugs

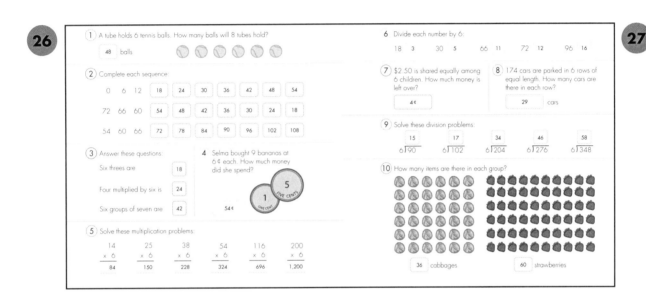

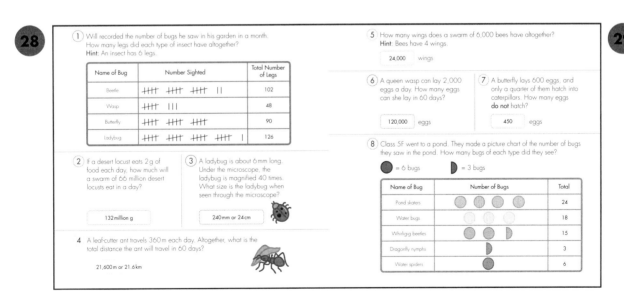

Children will be familiar with a range of tables and charts to represent data and use them to interpret and calculate information. The tables on these pages show a tally chart, using the "five bar gate" method of recording amounts, and a pictograph that uses an image to represent the data collected.

Answers:

30–31 Sports
32–33 Groups of 7

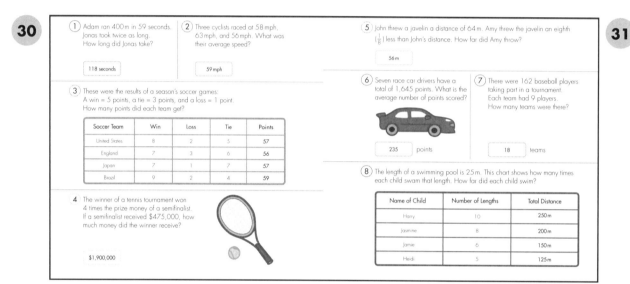

30

1. Adam ran 400 m in 59 seconds. Jonas took twice as long. How long did Jonas take?
118 seconds

2. Three cyclists raced at 58 mph, 63 mph, and 56 mph. What was their average speed?
59 mph

3. These were the results of a season's soccer games:
A win = 5 points, a tie = 3 points, and a loss = 1 point.
How many points did each team get?

Soccer Team	Win	Loss	Tie	Points
United States	8	2	5	57
England	7	3	6	56
Japan	7	1	7	57
Brazil	9	2	4	59

4. The winner of a tennis tournament won 4 times the prize money of a semifinalist. If a semifinalist received $475,000, how much money did the winner receive?
$1,900,000

31

5. John threw a javelin a distance of 64 m. Amy threw the javelin an eighth ($\frac{1}{8}$) less than John's distance. How far did Amy throw?
56 m

6. Seven race car drivers have a total of 1,645 points. What is the average number of points scored?
235 points

7. There were 162 baseball players taking part in a tournament. Each team had 9 players. How many teams were there?
18 teams

8. The length of a swimming pool is 25 m. This chart shows how many times each child swam that length. How far did each child swim?

Name of Child	Number of Lengths	Total Distance
Harry	10	250 m
Jasmine	8	200 m
Jamie	6	150 m
Heidi	5	125 m

These yellow pages are also themed and involve using a mix of times tables to solve the problems. Question 2 involves knowing ways to calculate averages. The amounts need to be added and then divided by the number of amounts, which is three in this question.

32

1. A dog eats 3 dog treats a day. How many treats will it eat in 7 days?
21 treats

2. Complete each sequence:
0 7 14 **21 28** 35 **42** 49 **56** 63
84 77 70 **63 56** 49 **42** 35 **28** 21
35 42 49 **56 63** 70 **77** 84 **91** 98

3. Answer these questions:
Seven sixes are **42**
Eight multiplied by seven is **56**
Five groups of seven are **35**

4. A train ticket costs $7. How much will 6 tickets cost?
$42

5. Solve these multiplication problems:

14	20	35	59	123	246
× 7	× 7	× 7	× 7	× 7	× 7
98	140	245	413	861	1,722

33

6. Divide each number by 7:
0 **0**   21 **3**   49 **7**   77 **11**   98 **14**

7. Seven books cost $35.84 altogether. If each book was the same price, what was the price of 1 book? **$5.12**

8. Solve these division problems:
12 7)84   **20** 7)140   **15** 7)105   **19** 7)133   **32** 7)224

9. Share 42 chairs equally around 7 tables. How many chairs will you keep around each table? **6** chairs

10. How many shapes are there in each group?
49   **21**

Some of the Time Fillers provide tips on how to calculate or check the answers to certain times tables. Knowing a variety of methods supports understanding of the concepts of multiplication and division.

Answers:

34–35 Days of the Week
36–37 Dice and Cards

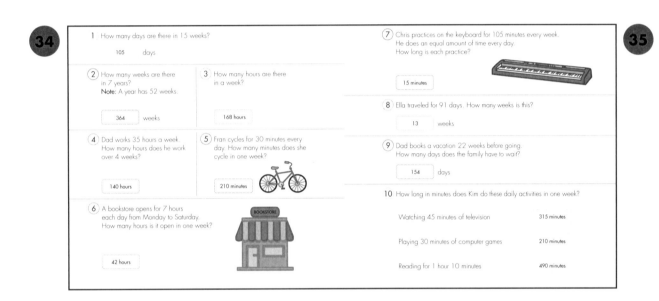

34

1 How many days are there in 15 weeks?

   105 days

2 How many weeks are there in 7 years?
   Note: A year has 52 weeks.

   364 weeks

3 How many hours are there in a week?

   168 hours

4 Dad works 35 hours a week. How many hours does he work over 4 weeks?

   140 hours

5 Fran cycles for 30 minutes every day. How many minutes does she cycle in one week?

   210 minutes

6 A bookstore opens for 7 hours each day from Monday to Saturday. How many hours is it open in one week?

   42 hours

35

7 Chris practices on the keyboard for 105 minutes every week. He does an equal amount of time every day. How long is each practice?

   15 minutes

8 Ella traveled for 91 days. How many weeks is this?

   13 weeks

9 Dad books a vacation 22 weeks before going. How many days does the family have to wait?

   154 days

10 How long in minutes does Kim do these daily activities in one week?

   Watching 45 minutes of television   315 minutes

   Playing 30 minutes of computer games   210 minutes

   Reading for 1 hour 10 minutes   490 minutes

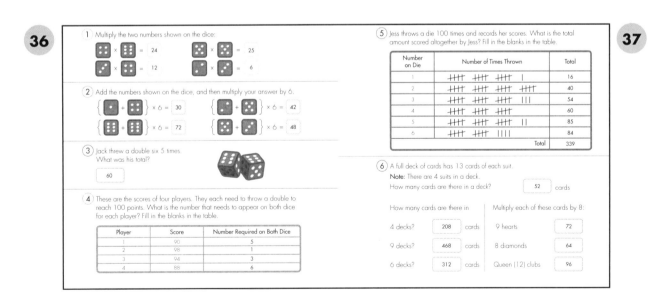

36

1 Multiply the two numbers shown on the dice:

   □ × □ = 24   □ × □ = 25

   □ × □ = 12   □ × □ = 6

2 Add the numbers shown on the dice, and then multiply your answer by 6.

   { □ + □ } × 6 = 30   { □ + □ } × 6 = 42

   { □ + □ } × 6 = 72   { □ + □ } × 6 = 48

3 Jack threw a double six 5 times. What was his total?

   60

4 These are the scores of four players. They each need to throw a double to reach 100 points. What is the number that needs to appear on both dice for each player? Fill in the blanks in the table.

Player	Score	Number Required on Both Dice
1	90	5
2	98	1
3	94	3
4	88	6

37

5 Jess throws a die 100 times and records her scores. What is the total amount scored altogether by Jess? Fill in the blanks in the table.

Number on Die	Number of Times Thrown	Total
1	ℍℍ ℍℍ ℍℍ I	16
2	ℍℍ ℍℍ ℍℍ ℍℍ	40
3	ℍℍ ℍℍ ℍℍ III	54
4	ℍℍ ℍℍ ℍℍ	60
5	ℍℍ ℍℍ ℍℍ II	85
6	ℍℍ ℍℍ IIII	84
	Total	339

6 A full deck of cards has 13 cards of each suit.
   Note: There are 4 suits in a deck.
   How many cards are there in a deck?   52 cards

   How many cards are there in   Multiply each of these cards by 8:

   4 decks?   208 cards   9 hearts   72

   9 decks?   468 cards   8 diamonds   64

   6 decks?   312 cards   Queen (12) clubs 96

Answers:

38–39 Groups of 8
40–41 Solar System

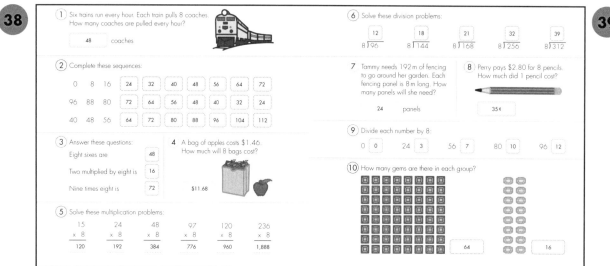

38

1. Six trains run every hour. Each train pulls 8 coaches. How many coaches are pulled every hour?

   48 coaches

2. Complete these sequences:

0	8	16	24	32	40	48	56	64	72

96	88	80	72	64	56	48	40	32	24

40	48	56	64	72	80	88	96	104	112

3. Answer these questions:

   Eight sixes are 48

   Two multiplied by eight is 16

   Nine times eight is 72

4. A bag of apples costs $1.46. How much will 8 bags cost?

   $11.68

5. Solve these multiplication problems:

15 × 8	24 × 8	48 × 8	97 × 8	120 × 8	236 × 8
120	192	384	776	960	1,888

39

6. Solve these division problems:

12 8⟌96	18 8⟌144	21 8⟌168	32 8⟌256	39 8⟌312

7. Tammy needs 192 m of fencing to go around her garden. Each fencing panel is 8 m long. How many panels will she need?

   24 panels

8. Perry pays $2.80 for 8 pencils. How much did 1 pencil cost?

   35¢

9. Divide each number by 8:

   0 [0]   24 [3]   56 [7]   80 [10]   96 [12]

10. How many gems are there in each group?

    64   16

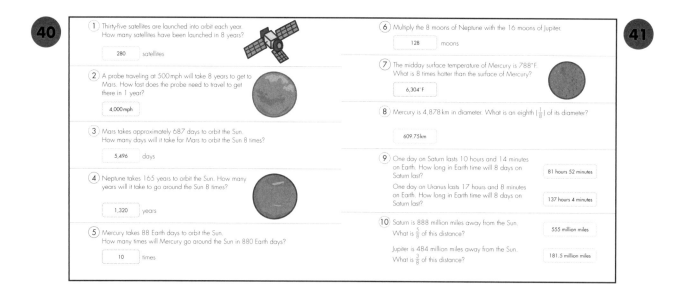

40

1. Thirty-five satellites are launched into orbit each year. How many satellites have been launched in 8 years?

   280 satellites

2. A probe traveling at 500 mph will take 8 years to get to Mars. How fast does the probe need to travel to get there in 1 year?

   4,000 mph

3. Mars takes approximately 687 days to orbit the Sun. How many days will it take for Mars to orbit the Sun 8 times?

   5,496 days

4. Neptune takes 165 years to orbit the Sun. How many years will it take to go around the Sun 8 times?

   1,320 years

5. Mercury takes 88 Earth days to orbit the Sun. How many times will Mercury go around the Sun in 880 Earth days?

   10 times

41

6. Multiply the 8 moons of Neptune with the 16 moons of Jupiter.

   128 moons

7. The midday surface temperature of Mercury is 788°F. What is 8 times hotter than the surface of Mercury?

   6,304°F

8. Mercury is 4,878 km in diameter. What is an eighth ($\frac{1}{8}$) of its diameter?

   609.75 km

9. One day on Saturn lasts 10 hours and 14 minutes on Earth. How long in Earth time will 8 days on Saturn last?

   81 hours 52 minutes

   One day on Uranus lasts 17 hours and 8 minutes on Earth. How long in Earth time will 8 days on Saturn last?

   137 hours 4 minutes

10. Saturn is 888 million miles away from the Sun. What is $\frac{5}{8}$ of this distance?

    555 million miles

    Jupiter is 484 million miles away from the Sun. What is $\frac{3}{8}$ of this distance?

    181.5 million miles

Answers:

42–43 Fractions
44–45 Groups of 9

42

① What is half ($\frac{1}{2}$) of each number?

18 **9**   10 **5**   6 **3**   24 **12**

② What is a third ($\frac{1}{3}$) of each amount?

12g **4g**   27g **9g**   33g **11g**   42g **14g**

3 What is a quarter ($\frac{1}{4}$) of each number?

4 **1**   20 **5**   36 **9**   52 **13**

④ There are 60 carrots in a box.
How many carrots make up…

$\frac{7}{10}$ of the box? **42** carrots

$\frac{1}{10}$ of the box? **6** carrots $\frac{2}{10}$ of the box? **12** carrots

⑤ There were 25 bananas, and $\frac{1}{5}$ were eaten.
How many bananas are left?

20 bananas

43

⑥ What is three quarters ($\frac{3}{4}$) of each number?

12 **9**   24 **18**   32 **24**   44 **33**

⑦ What is $\frac{1}{8}$ of 48 slices of pizza?

6 slices

⑧ What is $\frac{7}{10}$ of 40?

28

⑨ There are 30 children in a class. $\frac{3}{5}$ of the class have lunch in the cafeteria.
How many children **do not** have lunch in the cafeteria?

12 children

⑩ Oliver picked 54 apples. $\frac{1}{6}$ were rotten.
How many apples were rotten?

9 apples

At this level, children should be familiar with calculating fractions of amounts. Make sure they read the question carefully so that they don't get tricked by what the question is asking. For example,

Question 9 asks for the number of children who do not have school lunches, so they need to calculate $\frac{2}{5}$ of the 30 children.

44

① There are 8 horse races in a day. If 9 different horses took part in each race, how many horses ran that day?

72 horses

② Complete each sequence:

0 9 18 **27 36 45 54 63 72 81**

108 99 90 **81 72 63 54 45 36 27**

45 54 63 **72 81 90 99 108 117 126**

③ Answer these questions:

Three multiplied by nine is **27**

Nine eights are **72**

Six groups of nine are **54**

4 A bunch of flowers costs $4.99. How much will 9 bunches cost?

$44.91

⑤ Solve these multiplication problems:

16	23	92	47	150	218
× 9	× 9	× 9	× 9	× 9	× 9
144	**207**	**828**	**423**	**1,350**	**1,962**

45

⑥ Divide each number by 9:

9 **1**   36 **4**   45 **5**   90 **10**   108 **12**

⑦ Jake needed $468 to buy a new television. He decided to save an equal amount over 9 weeks to reach the total. What is the amount he needed to save each week?

$52

⑧ How many shapes are there in each group?

63   **18**

Answers:

46–47 Shopping
50–51 Division

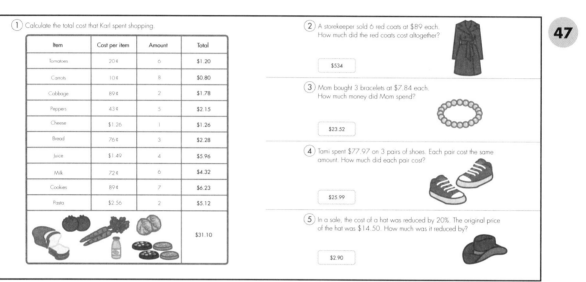

46

① Calculate the total cost that Karl spent shopping.

Item	Cost per item	Amount	Total
Tomatoes	20¢	6	$1.20
Carrots	10¢	8	$0.80
Cabbage	89¢	2	$1.78
Peppers	43¢	5	$2.15
Cheese	$1.26	1	$1.26
Bread	76¢	3	$2.28
Juice	$1.49	4	$5.96
Milk	72¢	6	$4.32
Cookies	89¢	7	$6.23
Pasta	$2.56	2	$5.12
			$31.10

47

② A storekeeper sold 6 red coats at $89 each. How much did the red coats cost altogether?

$534

③ Mom bought 3 bracelets at $7.84 each. How much money did Mom spend?

$23.52

④ Tami spent $77.97 on 3 pairs of shoes. Each pair cost the same amount. How much did each pair cost?

$25.99

⑤ In a sale, the cost of a hat was reduced by 20%. The original price of the hat was $14.50. How much was it reduced by?

$2.90

These pages demonstrate how multiplication and division skills are useful in shopping situations. Knowing how to calculate in sales price reductions can be very helpful while determining which products to buy.

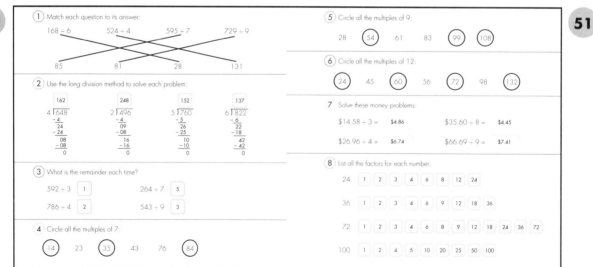

50

① Match each question to its answer:

168 ÷ 6   524 ÷ 4   595 ÷ 7   729 ÷ 9

85   81   28   131

② Use the long division method to solve each problem:

```
   162        248        152        137
4 ) 648    2 ) 496    5 ) 760    6 ) 822
  - 4        - 4        - 5        - 6
   24         09         26         22
  - 24       - 8        - 25       - 18
    08         16         10         42
   - 08       - 16       - 10       - 42
     0          0          0          0
```

③ What is the remainder each time?

592 ÷ 3   1   264 ÷ 7   5

786 ÷ 4   2   543 ÷ 9   3

④ Circle all the multiples of 7:

⑭   23   ㉟   43   76   ㉝

51

⑤ Circle all the multiples of 9:

28   ㊴   61   83   ㊟   ⑩⑧

⑥ Circle all the multiples of 12:

㉔   45   ㊉   56   ㉒   98   ⑬②

⑦ Solve these money problems:

$14.58 ÷ 3 = $4.86 $35.60 ÷ 8 = $4.45

$26.96 ÷ 4 = $6.74 $66.69 ÷ 9 = $7.41

⑧ List all the factors for each number:

24 | 1 | 2 | 3 | 4 | 6 | 8 | 12 | 24 |

36 | 1 | 2 | 3 | 4 | 6 | 9 | 12 | 18 | 36 |

72 | 1 | 2 | 3 | 4 | 6 | 8 | 9 | 12 | 18 | 24 | 36 | 72 |

100 | 1 | 2 | 4 | 5 | 10 | 20 | 25 | 50 | 100 |

Children may know either one method or a range of methods to easily divide multidigit whole numbers, such as the long division method. Also, they should be able to recognize factor pairs and the whole numbers as multiples of each of its factors.

Answers:

52–53 Groups of 11
54–55 Buildings

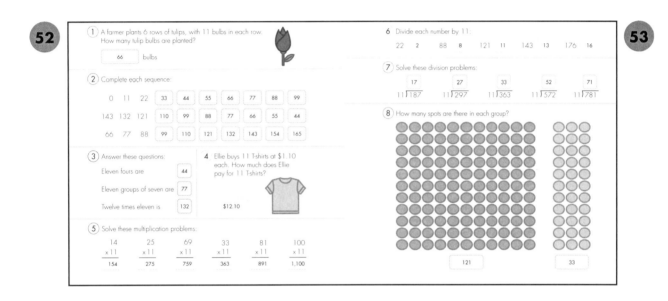

52

1 A farmer plants 6 rows of tulips, with 11 bulbs in each row. How many tulip bulbs are planted?

66 bulbs

2 Complete each sequence:

0	11	22	33	44	55	66	77	88	99
143	132	121	110	99	88	77	66	55	44
66	77	88	99	110	121	132	143	154	165

3 Answer these questions:

Eleven fours are **44**

Eleven groups of seven are **77**

Twelve times eleven is **132**

4 Ellie buys 11 T-shirts at $1.10 each. How much does Ellie pay for 11 T-shirts?

$12.10

5 Solve these multiplication problems:

14	25	69	33	81	100
×11	×11	×11	×11	×11	×11
154	275	759	363	891	1,100

53

6 Divide each number by 11:

22 **2**   88 **8**   121 **11**   143 **13**   176 **16**

7 Solve these division problems:

17	**27**	**33**	**52**	**71**
11)187	11)297	11)363	11)572	11)781

8 How many spots are there in each group?

121

33

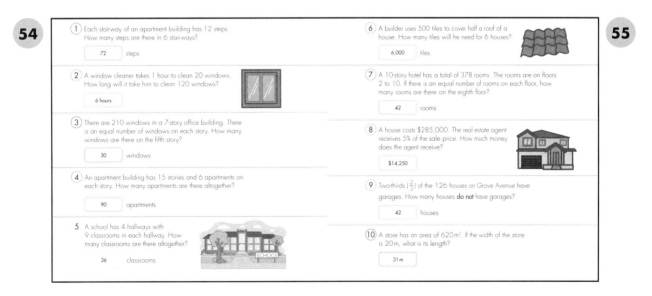

54

1 Each stairway of an apartment building has 12 steps. How many steps are there in 6 stairways?

72 steps

2 A window cleaner takes 1 hour to clean 20 windows. How long will it take him to clean 120 windows?

6 hours

3 There are 210 windows in a 7-story office building. There is an equal number of windows on each story. How many windows are there on the fifth story?

30 windows

4 An apartment building has 15 stories and 6 apartments on each story. How many apartments are there altogether?

90 apartments

5 A school has 4 hallways with 9 classrooms in each hallway. How many classrooms are there altogether?

36 classrooms

55

6 A builder uses 500 tiles to cover half a roof of a house. How many tiles will he need for 6 houses?

6,000 tiles

7 A 10-story hotel has a total of 378 rooms. The rooms are on floors 2 to 10. If there is an equal number of rooms on each floor, how many rooms are there on the eighth floor?

42 rooms

8 A house costs $285,000. The real estate agent receives 5% of the sale price. How much money does the agent receive?

$14,250

9 Two-thirds ($\frac{2}{3}$) of the 126 houses on Grove Avenue have garages. How many houses **do not** have garages?

42 houses

10 A store has an area of 620 m². If the width of the store is 20 m, what is its length?

31 m

Answers:

56–57 Sequences

58–59 Groups of 12

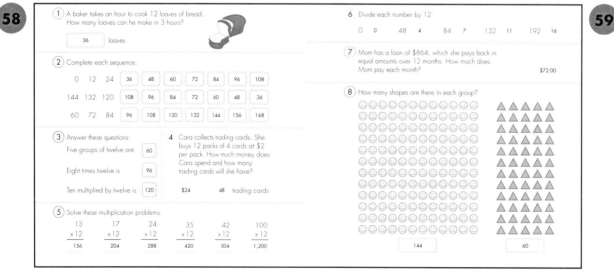

56

57

1. Fill in the missing numbers in each sequence:

| 5 | 10 | 15 | 20 | 25 | 30 | 35 | 40 | 45 | 50 |

| 60 | 65 | 70 | 75 | 80 | 85 | 90 | 95 | 100 | 105 |

2. Complete each sequence:

| 4 | 8 | 12 | 16 | 20 | 24 | 28 | 32 | 36 | 40 |

| 7 | 14 | 21 | 28 | 35 | 42 | 49 | 56 | 63 | 70 |

| 25 | 50 | 75 | 100 | 125 | 150 | 175 | 200 | 225 | 250 |

3. Continue this pattern:

4. Complete this chart:

×	0	1	2	3	4	5	6	7	8	9	10
6	0	6	12	18	24	30	36	42	48	54	60
9	0	9	18	27	36	45	54	63	72	81	90

5. Fill in the missing numbers in each sequence:

| 80 | 72 | 64 | 56 | 48 | 40 | 32 | 24 | 16 | 8 |

| 60 | 56 | 52 | 48 | 44 | 40 | 36 | 32 | 28 | 24 |

6. Continue this pattern:

7. Complete this chart:

×	10	9	8	7	6	5	4	3	2	1	0
11	110	99	88	77	66	55	44	33	22	11	0
12	120	108	96	84	72	60	48	36	24	12	0

8. Complete each sequence:

| 200 | 190 | 180 | 170 | 160 | 150 | 140 | 130 | 120 | 110 |

| 150 | 148 | 146 | 144 | 142 | 140 | 138 | 136 | 134 | 132 |

These sequences identify multiples of times tables and also the patterns between numbers.

58

59

1. A baker takes an hour to cook 12 loaves of bread. How many loaves can he make in 3 hours?

36 loaves

2. Complete each sequence:

| 0 | 12 | 24 | 36 | 48 | 60 | 72 | 84 | 96 | 108 |

| 144 | 132 | 120 | 108 | 96 | 84 | 72 | 60 | 48 | 36 |

| 60 | 72 | 84 | 96 | 108 | 120 | 132 | 144 | 156 | 168 |

3. Answer these questions:

Five groups of twelve are 60

Eight times twelve is 96

Ten multiplied by twelve is 120

4. Cara collects trading cards. She buys 12 packs of 4 cards at $2 per pack. How much money does Cara spend and how many trading cards will she have?

$24   48 trading cards

5. Solve these multiplication problems.

13	17	24	35	42	100
×12	×12	×12	×12	×12	×12
156	204	288	420	504	1,200

6. Divide each number by 12:

| 0 | 0 | 48 | 4 | 84 | 7 | 132 | 11 | 192 | 16 |

7. Mom has a loan of $864, which she pays back in equal amounts over 12 months. How much does Mom pay each month?

$72.00

8. How many shapes are there in each group?

144   60

Answers:

60–61 Dozen a Day
62–63 Plants

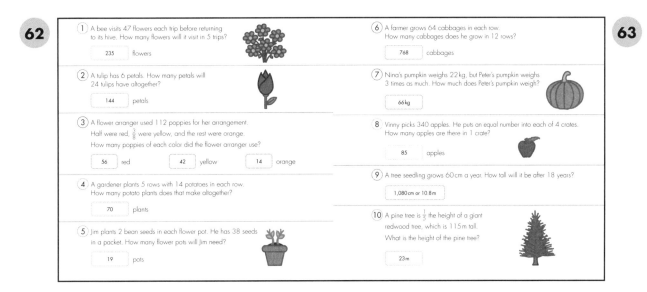

60

1. A dozen children split themselves equally into 3 teams to play a game. How many children are there in each team?

   4 children

2. Cupcakes were sold in boxes of 12. How many cupcakes were there in 15 boxes?

   180 cupcakes

3. How many dozen eggs are there in a gross of eggs? **Hint:** A gross is 144.

   12 dozen

4. What are the factors of 12?

   1   2   3   4   6   12

5. A score of children had 12 candies each. How many candies did they have altogether? **Note:** A score is 20.

   240 candies

61

6. A chef cooks a batch of 12 pancakes in 12 minutes. How many batches of 12 pancakes can he make in an hour?

   5 batches

7. Trains arrived at Whistlestop Station 3 times an hour. How many trains arrived in 12 hours?

   36 trains

8. A group of musicians performed a dozen pieces in a concert. Each piece lasted 4 minutes. How many minutes did the musicians perform altogether?

   48 minutes

9. 900 raffle tickets were sold at a fund-raising event. There were a dozen prizes. What was the chance of winning a prize? Circle the correct answer.

   1 in 50   (1 in 75)   1 in 100

10. Once a month, Jill ran a distance of 5,000 meters in a cross-country event. How many meters did Jill run in a year?

    60,000 meters

62

1. A bee visits 47 flowers each trip before returning to its hive. How many flowers will it visit in 5 trips?

   235 flowers

2. A tulip has 6 petals. How many petals will 24 tulips have altogether?

   144 petals

3. A flower arranger used 112 poppies for her arrangement. Half were red, $\frac{3}{8}$ were yellow, and the rest were orange. How many poppies of each color did the flower arranger use?

   56 red   **42** yellow   **14** orange

4. A gardener plants 5 rows with 14 potatoes in each row. How many potato plants does that make altogether?

   70 plants

5. Jim plants 2 bean seeds in each flower pot. He has 38 seeds in a packet. How many flower pots will Jim need?

   19 pots

63

6. A farmer grows 64 cabbages in each row. How many cabbages does he grow in 12 rows?

   768 cabbages

7. Nina's pumpkin weighs 22 kg, but Peter's pumpkin weighs 3 times as much. How much does Peter's pumpkin weigh?

   66 kg

8. Vinny picks 340 apples. He puts an equal number into each of 4 crates. How many apples are there in 1 crate?

   85 apples

9. A tree seedling grows 60 cm a year. How tall will it be after 18 years?

   1,080 cm or 10.8 m

10. A pine tree is $\frac{1}{5}$ the height of a giant redwood tree, which is 115 m tall. What is the height of the pine tree?

    23 m

Answers:

24–25 Beat the Clock 1
48–49 Beat the Clock 2
64–65 Beat the Clock 3

These Beat the Clock pages test your child's ability to quickly recall times tables facts. The tests require your child to work under some pressure. As with most tests of this type, tell children before they start not to get stuck on one question, but to move on and return to the tricky one later if time allows. Encourage your child to record his/her score and the time taken to complete the test, then to retake the test later to see if he/she can improve on their previous attempt.

24 / 25

#		#		#		#		#		#	
1	0	2	24	3	45	31	8	32	3	33	3
4	4	5	55	6	12	34	6	35	3	36	3
7	21	8	20	9	4	37	7	38	1	39	5
10	30	11	44	12	16	40	8	41	1	42	9
13	16	14	50	15	10	43	7	44	2	45	1
16	18	17	90	18	36	46	9	47	9	48	8
19	5	20	48	21	24	49	3	50	5	51	6
22	28	23	10	24	120	52	5	53	12	54	7
25	8	26	70	27	100	55	6	56	12	57	11
28	32	29	22	30	0	58	10	59	5	60	10

48 / 49

#		#		#		#		#		#	
1	0	2	0	3	72	31	0	32	10	33	7
4	40	5	56	6	24	34	0	35	11	36	12
7	18	8	42	9	14	37	1	38	3	39	6
10	7	11	81	12	90	40	1	41	12	42	9
13	16	14	8	15	72	43	3	44	4	45	9
16	18	17	63	18	70	46	4	47	5	48	5
19	28	20	36	21	66	49	11	50	8	51	6
22	64	23	48	24	88	52	10	53	7	54	2
25	54	26	42	27	84	55	6	56	8	57	8
28	30	29	49	30	108	58	5	59	9	60	12

64 / 65

#		#		#		#		#		#	
1	27	2	76	3	120	31	6	32	49	33	17
4	7	5	108	6	96	34	9	35	14	36	8
7	24	8	80	9	60	37	7	38	20	39	46
10	20	11	0	12	22	40	8	41	18	42	21
13	40	14	66	15	54	43	7	44	456	45	14
16	16	17	48	18	32	46	13	47	179	48	38
19	49	20	50	21	0	49	10	50	86	51	9
22	21	23	135	24	32	52	5	53	20	54	32
25	3	26	136	27	190	55	17	56	13	57	12
28	20	29	105	30	192	58	16	59	11	60	100